Contents

Introduction		1
Prayer of Commitment		3
Session 1	A New Identity	3
Session 2	Creation and Chaos	15
Session 3	From Liberation to Slavery	23
	The Bible: An Overview	34
Session 4	A Surprising Deliverance	37
Session 5	Following the Master	47
Session 6	New Habits, New Gifts, and a New Me	57
Next Steps		67

Introduction

This course is designed for those who have made a commitment to Jesus Christ and are now Christians. It is an introduction to the Christian faith, and was written to give new Christians an understanding of their new identity, their history, their Bible, and their future. However, it can also be used by more experienced Christians who want to revisit and rediscover the foundations of their faith. The course was originally commissioned by Steve Abley, Director of Burn 24/7, to be used in conjunction with their programme for new believers. If you are part of this programme, then you will be working through this with a mentor. If not, then we would strongly recommend working through this with a more mature Christian, either one-to-one, or with a group of two or three others. This person could meet with you for each session, read through the material with you, answer questions, facilitate discussion, pray with you, and walk with you through the first few months of your newfound faith.

Lucy Peppiatt & **Matthew Lynch**

Prayer of commitment

If you are a new believer, you might have prayed a prayer like this one below. You may find it helpful to look back at this prayer to recall the kind of commitment you have made:

> Dear Lord Jesus, I have heard that your love never fails, that you are willing to forgive, that you have power to heal. I have heard that before I knew you, you knew me, you loved me and you gave yourself for me.
>
> Today, I want to know and experience your love for me. So I turn towards your kindness and forgiveness with my deepest needs and my deepest wounds.
>
> I pray, Lord Jesus Christ, have mercy on me, and forgive me. Pour your healing love into my life and make me new. Show me the way to go and I will follow.
>
> Amen.

SESSION 1
A New Identity

Becoming a Christian is not just about believing something new, it's about becoming *someone* new.

The Bible readings in this course introduce you to key biblical themes and ideas, and complement each session. The sessions are not necessarily 'Bible studies' on the readings, so just enjoy them! Your mentor can also help you understand parts of these Bible chapters that you find challenging.

**John 1:1-14
Romans 8 & 12**

A new adventure

Meeting Jesus for the first time (or re-connecting with him again) is a life-changing experience. It probably feels exciting and a bit scary all at the same time. You may not be entirely sure what you have done! Having trusted and believed that Jesus has taken away your sin and has given you a new life, you may feel there is a lot you still do not know about your faith, who you have become, and what that looks like in practice. There is a lot to learn and discover, and this is the start of a great adventure!

Knowing God

Entering a relationship with God is the most amazing and fascinating experience you can ever have. You are getting to know the One who made you in the first place, who knows you inside and out, who loves you more than you can imagine, and who has great plans for your life. The more time and energy you invest in getting to know God the more you will grow in Him and enjoy your new life. Once you encounter God through Jesus Christ and the Holy Spirit, you find that He is captivating.

Read and discover

- The One who made you (Genesis 1:26-31)
- The One who knows and guides you (Psalm 139:1-10)
- The One who has great plans for you (Jeremiah 29:11-13)

Jesus the Saviour

The Son of God came to earth as Jesus of Nazareth (his hometown in Israel) to save humankind. Because he loved us so much, and while we were still sinners, he came to seek and to save the lost (Luke 19:10), to rescue us from sin and evil, and to bring us into his Kingdom (Colossians 1:13).

All we have to do to receive his forgiveness, salvation, and healing is to recognize that we are the ones who are lost and who need saving, and to put our trust in the power and reality of Jesus' death and resurrection to save us. We respond to his invitation to give our lives to him, by offering him ourselves.

We are assuming that you have prayed a prayer saying sorry to God and giving your life to him (like the 'Prayer of Commitment' found on page 4). It is through Jesus and the Holy Spirit that we come into a relationship with our Heavenly Father.

Talk to your mentor about how you came to give your life to Jesus.

NOTES

Becoming someone new

Becoming a Christian is not just about believing something new, it's about becoming *someone* new. Sometimes Christians talk about new birth, as if we are actually starting life all over again - something Jesus himself talked about (John 3:3-7). This begins when we give our allegiance to *Jesus Christ as Lord*. We declare that he is Lord, or King, over the whole universe, and we embrace him as Lord of our lives. This means that we give our lives to him, trusting that he *is* the truth. What he taught his disciples was true for them, and is true for us. So we begin to follow his teaching, trusting that he knows what is best for us. This process makes us into someone new. Becoming and being a Christian is all about Jesus bringing us into a relationship with the Father in the power of the Holy Spirit.

The Bible talks about being 'in Christ', 'clothed with Christ', 'belonging to Christ', and going 'into Christ'. These are all ways to tell us that in our relationship with Jesus, he is always *with* us, always *for* us, and always *in* us. We have a new best friend who will never let us down.

> "Therefore, if anyone is in Christ, the new creation has come: The old has gone, the new is here!"
> **(2 Corinthians 5:17)**

> "So in Christ Jesus you are all children of God through faith, for all of you who were baptized into Christ have clothed yourselves with Christ." **(Galatians 3:26-27)**

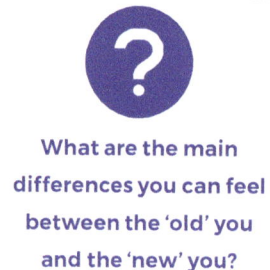

What are the main differences you can feel between the 'old' you and the 'new' you?

NOTES

Living in a new country

In the reading from John's Gospel we discover that we have the 'right' to be called children of God (John 1:12-13). He has adopted us into his family. As God's children, we also discover the right to claim one of the greatest spiritual blessings a person could ever have: a relationship with God as our Father. This is not only a gift. It is our right when we commit our lives to Jesus. And if we are children of God, then we gain access to the riches of heaven, not because we deserve it, but because our Father lovingly gives it. From Him we inherit the Kingdom of God.

Our new life takes us into a new identity and access to a new Kingdom, like getting a new nationality and a new passport. We are now living in God's country, His Kingdom, where we have all the rights and privileges of this country's citizens.

This is a Kingdom of light, forgiveness, healing, power, glory, and cleansing. It is a Kingdom of God's riches, which are love, joy, and peace. This is what we are given as children of God.

What would you like to claim as part of your inheritance as a child of God?

NOTES

God's ambassadors

We also become ambassadors for this country, representing God in everything we do, and telling other people about this fantastic new life that they can have too, if they want it.

> *"We are therefore Christ's ambassadors, as though God were making his appeal through us. We implore you on Christ's behalf: Be reconciled to God."*
> **(2 Corinthians 5:20)**

Think of someone who might need reconciliation with God. Could God be leading you to make an appeal for them to be reconciled? Pray for them and then go ahead and speak with them about Him!

Life together

You will already have met your mentor and will be getting to know them. The Christian life has to be lived with others because there is no such thing as a lone Christian. The Bible calls this 'fellowship'. It is deeper than just friendship, and is more like a family, where we stay with each other through thick and thin. Christians all share the same heavenly Father, and every other Christian is now our brother or sister. This is the church. So we become part of the church whether we want to or not! You may often read the Bible, worship, and pray at home, on your own, but being part of a church means that you also do those things in a community. You are designed to grow as a Christian in the company and friendship of others. So do join a church and make Christian friends.

A Christian is no longer just an 'I'. They are also part of a 'we', because God's plan is to create a community in which his Spirit - or Presence - can come to be with His people.

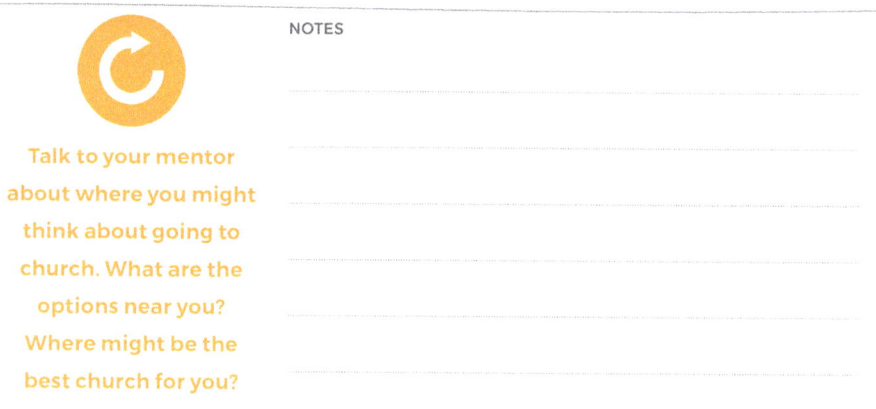

Talk to your mentor about where you might think about going to church. What are the options near you? Where might be the best church for you?

NOTES

One of the things that we teach at Westminster Theological Centre is that God is always at work, creating a **people** and a **place** for His **presence**. Christians are united by their shared belief in one God, their new identity as little 'Christs', their baptism, and because the same Holy Spirit lives in all of us. We all live in the presence of the same God.

Same but different

We are all one family, but we do not all worship in the same way. All over the world, and in different churches, we use different languages, music styles, prayers, and ways to express our commitment and love for God. You will join a church that does things differently from the church down the road, and that's fine! It is good to have diversity as long as we remember that in reality we are all one family. In spite of everything that makes us different, there are three things that all Christians share: one is a prayer, one is a statement of what we believe - a creed - and one is baptism. These are part of our new family identity and values: our shared prayer, our shared creed, and our one baptism.

Christians are all baptised in the name of the Father, the Son, and the Holy Spirit. This is the sign of our new identity. The water symbolises how we die to our old ways by going down into the waters of death. By this we share in Christ's death. But the waters also symbolise cleansing from Christ. With Him, we rise up from the waters to new life and the promise of resurrection after death. That water also symbolizes your connection to Christians around the world, who also went through the waters to new life. If you are not baptised, you can use this course as a preparation for your baptism.

Prayer is another important part of the Christian life. When we pray we talk to God and listen for His voice. Here is the prayer that Jesus taught his disciples when they asked him how to pray:

> **THE LORD'S PRAYER**
> *Our Father in heaven,*
> *hallowed be your name.*
> *Your kingdom come,*
> *your will be done,*
> *on earth as in heaven.*
> *Give us today our daily bread.*
> *Forgive us our sins,*
> *as we forgive those who sin against us.*
> *Lead us not into temptation,*
> *but deliver us from evil.*
> *For the kingdom,*
> *the power and the glory are yours.*
> *Now and for ever.*
> *Amen.*

If you look carefully at the Lord's Prayer you will see that the first part is about God, the second part is about us. What does this teach us about how we should pray?

NOTES

Belief is another key part of the Christian life. Christians share several core beliefs about Jesus. Here is an ancient statement of belief that all Christians can agree on. Don't worry if you don't understand all the language here straight away. It can sound a bit strange, but there were reasons why ancient Christians used the language that they did. You can talk about this with your mentor and your minister, pastor, or vicar, or leave it for later!

Why do you think it is important that the Church has a statement of belief in the Creed?

NOTES

THE NICENE CREED

We believe in one God,

the Father, the Almighty,

maker of heaven and earth,

of all that is, seen and unseen.

We believe in one Lord, Jesus Christ,

the only Son of God,

eternally begotten of the Father,

God from God, Light from Light,

true God from true God,

begotten, not made,

of one Being with the Father.

Through him all things were made.

For us and for our salvation

he came down from heaven:

by the power of the Holy Spirit

he became incarnate from the Virgin Mary,

and was made man.

For our sake he was crucified under Pontius Pilate;

he suffered death and was buried.

On the third day he rose again

in accordance with the Scriptures;

he ascended in heaven

and is seated at the right hand of the Father.

He will come again in glory to judge the living and the dead,

and his kingdom will have no end.

We believe in the Holy Spirit, the Lord, the giver of life,

who proceeds from the Father and the Son.

With the Father and the Son he is worshiped and glorified.

He has spoken through the Prophets.

We believe in one holy catholic[1] and apostolic Church.

We acknowledge one baptism for the forgiveness of sins.

We look for the resurrection of the dead,

and the life of the world to come.

Amen.

FOOTNOTE 1
The word 'catholic' in the creed means worldwide or universal. It refers to our connection with all believers everywhere.

Knowing your story

We have talked so far about our shared prayer and our shared creed. Christians also share a book – the Bible. The Bible is a big story that stretches back to the beginning of all creation and reaches forward to the hope of a New Creation, when God will re-create and heal everything He has made. Since all Christians share this book - this story – it will be helpful to learn its basic plotline and 'big idea'. We might summarise both by returning to the wording used earlier: *God is at work creating a* **people** *and a* **place** *for his* **presence**. As you grow in your faith, you will find that you want to know the story more deeply, and that it becomes your story.

One of the reasons that Christians place such importance on the Bible is that it is God's way of speaking to us - God's word to the world. Although the perfect revelation of God comes to us in Jesus Christ (who is the Word of God according to John 1), the Bible is how God has chosen to reveal His character and His purposes to us in written form. For this reason, it is unique. Think of the Bible as God reaching out to you to build a relationship with you. As God reaches out, He tells you about your new identity in Christ. Your story is now going to be shaped by Jesus and his story. So, we want you to understand the story of him and his people - the people you are now part of.

Looking ahead

The next three sessions look at the big story of the whole Bible, describing it like a grand drama with 7 Episodes, each with its own twists and turns. Seeing the Bible as a drama helps us to understand our place in the story. As you will later discover, the world we live in today falls between Episode 6 & Episode 7, between the time when restoration begins in Christ and when God's work in creation reaches its fullness. But at different times in our lives we will also identify with different parts of the story, and as we do this, the Bible comes alive. The Bible's stories reveal deep truths to us about God, ourselves, others, and the world.

NOTES

SESSION 2

Creation and Chaos

We now turn to look at **the big story of the whole Bible.** This will help you to know more about **God's great plan** for the world, to know your **Christian history** and to help you to **begin to read your Bible.**

We have included a helpful Bible Overview spread on pp.36-37 which can aid you in your reading by showing where the individual books fit into the bigger structure of the Bible.

Genesis 1-3 & 12

Putting the pieces together

The Bible is quite long! But it was not all written at the same time. Nor is it just one book. It is actually a collection of books - 66 to be precise - with 39 in the Old Testament and 27 in the New Testament (see p. 34–35). The Bible is a mini library of books that were written over a span of roughly 1,000 years. So, reading *straight through* the Bible can sometimes be a bumpy ride, jolting you from stories to laws, from wise sayings to poetry, and from prophecies to letters - and all of these from different times in history.

Not surprisingly, reading the Bible can be exhilarating and disorientating! But as you slow down you may begin to see how the parts fit together. Think of the parts like the shoots of a runner plant. The shoots might *appear* disconnected, but when you dig into the soil you see how they are linked. In fact, the links are so many that we can begin to see the Bible as a big, unified story of God, His people, and the world He loves.

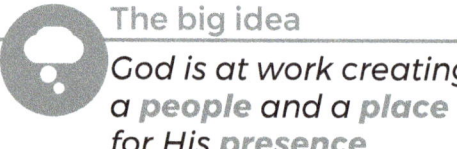

The big idea
God is at work creating a people *and a* place *for His* presence.

As we mentioned in Session 1, one way of thinking about the **big idea** of this story is as follows: *God is at work creating a people and a place for His presence*. There are a few key things to notice about this summary.

First, the Bible is a story about what *God* is doing. He is the main actor in the story, and getting to know His character changes everything.

Second, it is a story about what God is doing with a *people*. This means that we are not meant to be alone, but part of something bigger. The main way that the Bible speaks about this is through the metaphor of *family*. God adopts us into His family, where we call each other brother and sister, and discover that we are all beloved children of God.

Third, this is a story about a *place*. In the Bible, that place is the world. From beginning (Genesis 1-2) to end (Revelation 21-22), the Bible tells us that God 'so loved the world' (John 3:16). He loves it so much that He wants us to appreciate it, protect it, and ultimately, He wants to redeem it – and make it new. But God also cares about the little places. He cares about our homes, our neighbourhoods, and our communities, and He wants us to *find our place* in the world.

Fourth, the Bible is a story about God constantly seeking to be present with His people. Jesus says that 'where two or three gather in my name, there am I with them' (Matthew 18:20).

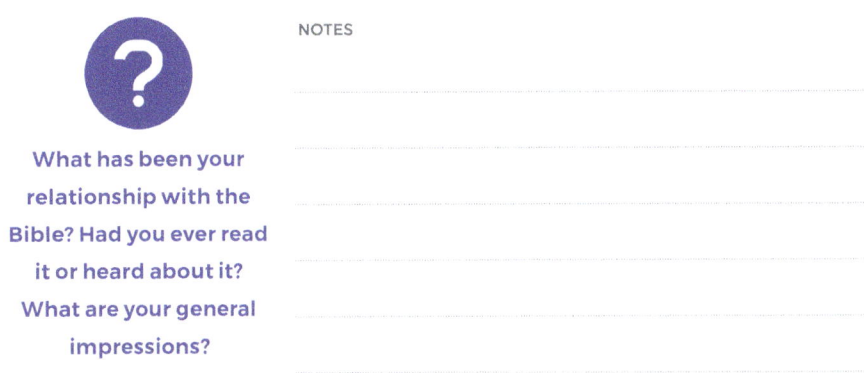

What has been your relationship with the Bible? Had you ever read it or heard about it? What are your general impressions?

NOTES

Episode 1: A New World

From the beginning we meet a God who is creative and generous. He creates a good world and invites humanity to share in His rule by developing and caring for the world, and by reflecting His presence into the world. The world God makes is a place of *shalom*, a Hebrew term meaning right-relating wholeness. That *shalom* is what God desires for His relationships with us, between humans, and with the world.

God loves creation. In Genesis 1 alone, God states *seven times* that creation is 'good.' God is an artist, delighted with His work: 'God saw all that he had made, and behold, it was very good' (Genesis 1:31). The delighted artist made humans 'in the image of God' (Genesis 1:26-28). This means that a) God's presence shines through you; b) *you* are of inestimable worth; and c) *you* share in God's rule and life. An image is literally a 'living icon' of God. A living icon points to God but also reflects the light of God out into the world. We were made for God and for the world. We enjoy life with God by the presence of His Spirit and are responsible for ruling like our loving God.

Part of that responsibility involves creating communities and cultivating the earth. 'Being fruitful and multiplying' is the biblical phrase for this. Genesis 1-2 reveals that the world is *not yet* what God desires it to become. It is *not yet* filled, *not yet* cultivated, and *not yet* developed into all that it could be. This is an important starting point for understanding the grand biblical story. The world is *good* but not yet complete. There is more to the big story, just as there is more to your story. God made the world for development and change, and made humans to be creative as they unlock its potential. But things get worse before they get better.

Discuss how being made in God's image might affect the way you see yourself and others.

NOTES

Episode 2: The Loss of Wholeness

Genesis 3 is an important chapter in the Bible. Earlier, God had placed humans in a garden called Eden and told them not to eat of the 'tree of the knowledge of good and evil' (Genesis 2:17). This tree represented the pursuit of autonomy, power, and godlikeness. Eating from it would lead to death. But against this command, and with the deceptive influence of a crafty serpent, humans decided to eat from it. By eating, they chose to define goodness for themselves. This act led to their expulsion from the garden where God had placed them, leaving them without access to the garden's other tree, the tree of life (Genesis 3:22-23).

From here on in, things spiral out of control. The sickness of sin infected all humanity and sets them on a path of death. A catastrophic flood in Genesis 6-9 shows us that the problems of sin and death had reached into every corner of the world. Human violence had spiralled out of control until everything collapsed and returned to its pre-creation state of watery chaos. But even then, God was *present*.

He preserved His creation and representatives of humanity in a boat, which floated along safely 'over the surface of the waters' (Genesis 7:18) just as God's Spirit had hovered 'over the surface of the waters' in the beginning (Genesis 1:2). This is a God who renews and makes new, no matter how bad things get.

Ask the Spirit to help you identify places that need to be made new. Perhaps those are within you, in your family, or in your neighbourhood. Write down one way that you can participate in that renewal and discuss it with your mentor.

NOTES

Episode 3: Abraham and the Chosen Family

By Genesis 11, humanity had already reverted back to its sinful ways. This time, they tried to become like God by constructing a huge imperial city with a tower reaching into heaven. This city, named Babylon (*Babel* in Hebrew), could have been a total disaster. Oppressive and arrogant kingdoms trample people - and they still do. Humans are made for building homes, neighbourhoods, and communities. We are made for sharing and not hoarding power. So God intervened again to prevent humans from grasping after power.

But God's response was not only reactive. He was proactive. He set to work addressing the underlying problems of sin and death that plagued humanity and threatened the world. His solution was surprising - to say the least! He chose an elderly migrant couple named Abraham and Sarah, who were unable to have children, and made them an extraordinary promise:

*"Go from your country [Babylon], your people and your father's household and go to the **land** I will show you. I will make you into a **great nation**, and I will bless you; I will make your name great, and you will be a blessing. I will bless those who bless you, and whoever curses you I will curse; and all peoples on earth will be blessed through you."* **(Genesis 12:1-3, emphasis added)**

This is God's way. He chooses the unlikely, the vulnerable, those without privilege, and partners with them - with you! - to bring about His purposes. God promised that through *this* elderly couple and their offspring, He would bless all the nations. Moreover, He would give this family's descendants a land where they could learn to live God's way. But this calling required **trust**. Abraham had to uproot from Babylon, leave his family, and settle in an unknown and faraway land. That land was called Canaan, and was later renamed Israel.

The plan was that by living God's way in a **land** He gave them, the nations would learn God's beautiful way of living. This was to be characterized by *shalom* (right-relating wholeness). Israel's later prophets prophesied about what this would look like:

"[God] will judge between the nations and will settle disputes for many peoples. They will beat their swords into ploughshares and their spears into pruning hooks. Nation will not take up sword against nation, nor will they train for war anymore." **(Isaiah 2:4)**

God's covenant

God chose Abraham's family to show and then teach the nations God's ideals of *shalom*. God promised that through Abraham and Sarah, He would form a people to embody His original purposes for humanity who, by living in faithfulness, would bring blessing to the world. God then sealed His promises to Abraham through a **covenant**, a binding agreement to remain faithful and present. God's promise to keep His covenant was so rock solid that He swore *on his own life* to keep it (Genesis 15)!

There is even a special Hebrew word to describe God's never-ending guaranteed faithfulness to keep His covenant with His people. That covenant faithfulness is called *chesed* (spoken with a guttural *ch*, like Ba*ch*), sometimes translated as 'steadfast love.' This steadfast love is the drumbeat of the Bible. 'His steadfast love endures forever … His steadfast love endures forever … [and 24 more times!]' sings the psalmist in Psalm 136. This is a God who keeps His promises, and whose life is bound up with the lives of His people.

If it is true that God has bound Himself to humans in steadfast love and faithfulness, how does the idea of covenant affect your view of God and the biblical story?

SESSION 2

NOTES

SESSION 3

From Liberation to Slavery

The rest of the Old Testament and into the New Testament follows **the story of Israel.**

Exodus 1-3 & 19
Lamentations 1

Moving forward

In Session 2, we looked at the first three episodes of the biblical drama, all of which take place in the first book of the Bible, Genesis. As you follow the story into the second book, Exodus, you will notice that the *family* of Abraham has grown into a **people** - Israel (named after Abraham's grandson Jacob/Israel). The story of Israel is told through the rest of the Old Testament, and into the New Testament. They are the people God has chosen to redeem humanity and creation. Redemption (literally 'buying back') is central to how God works. He redeems His people in order to restore them to wholeness. God does this not because He found Israel to be superior in its holiness, but because He loved them and delighted in choosing this small and weak nation to reveal His power. That was His plan! But for much of the story the plan seems to have gone awry, even from the very beginnings of Israel as a people in Egypt.

Episode 4: Exodus and the Chosen People

So far in our story, God has created a good world, but it became infected with a decaying malady called sin. God's response was to choose Abraham's family. He promised that through them he would bless and redeem the world. God re-affirmed his covenant with Isaac - Abraham and Sarah's son - and then Jacob, whose name became Israel (Genesis 32). By the end of Genesis, God's chosen family had grown from a few to a much larger family of 70 in all. But due to famine, Jacob's family ended up in Egypt for *400 years*, at the end of which they were enslaved by 'the mean Pharaoh', as Matt's 4-year-old daughter put it.

Things looked grim for the people of Israel. They were enslaved, downtrodden, and without any hope. So they did what all people do in such circumstances. *They cried out.* Their cry reached God. And like so many of our cries, it seemed to go unanswered ... until, God surprised one particular Israelite named Moses, who had fled from Egypt and was living in the wilderness. God appeared to Moses in a burning bush (yes, he was surprised too!) and said to him:

> *"I have indeed seen the misery of my people in Egypt. I have **heard** them crying out because of their slave drivers, and I am **concerned about** their suffering. So I have **come down** to **rescue** them from the hand of the Egyptians and to **bring them up** out of that land into a good and spacious land, a land flowing with milk and honey."* **(Exodus 3:7-8)**

Notice the movement here. God does not remain in heaven, waiting for us to climb up to Him, or to become a spiritual superhero. Instead, He comes *down* because He is responsive to the cries of the afflicted, the tears of the oppressed, and the groans of the weary. But His arrival does not only bring humanitarian aid and relief. He also restores human dignity, by bringing his people *forward*, into something new, into a good land. He wants the downcast to lift their heads. Leviticus (the third Old Testament book) puts it beautifully:

> *"I am the LORD your God, who brought you out of Egypt so that you would no longer be slaves to the Egyptians; **I broke the bars of your yoke and enabled you to walk with heads held high.**"* **(Leviticus 26:13)**

So God did rescue his people from Egypt - the most powerful nation on earth at the time - and brought them to a good land.

SESSION 3

There are people crying out in our society. Think about how you can attune your ears to the cries of others and how to respond.

NOTES

At the mountain with God

Before God's people arrived in the land He had promised them, He brought them to Mount Sinai, and there He made a covenant with them (the **Sinai Covenant**). The earlier covenant with Abraham, Isaac, and Jacob was still in effect, but it did not include any details about what God expected from His people once they became a nation. In addition, the Israelites had been so dehumanised during their time in Egypt that they needed to learn how to live again. So, God gave them instructions (sometimes called 'the Torah,' or 'the law') to show them how to live with each other and with Him. Most importantly, these instructions showed Israel how to worship God and enjoy His intimate presence. This was all part of God's plan to create a people and a place for His **presence**.

Into a new land

Then God brought His people into the land of Canaan (later renamed Israel). In that land, they matured and developed as a nation. They were still small, and pressed in on every side by the superpowers of the ancient world. They had Egypt to the west, the Hittites to the north, and the Assyrians and the Babylonians to the east. They were a 'land bridge,' small and trampled by their more powerful neighbours, but of infinite worth to God. In time, and because of external military pressures, Israel asked for a king to help build an army to protect them from attacks. This was not God's plan. *He* was to be their king. And Israel was supposed to be a community of brothers and sisters, without anyone assuming a higher status (see Deuteronomy 18).

Nevertheless, God granted their wish for a king, and worked with Israel where they were at. God even established a covenant with Israel's second major king, David. This became known as the **Davidic Covenant**. In this covenant, God promised to maintain His steadfast love toward David and his descendants, always keeping one of them on the throne in Jerusalem. This king would be like a shepherd over God's people, looking after the weakest members and protecting the whole flock.

But even more, God was promising to fulfil His purposes *for Israel* through the Davidic King whom He called to live in faithfulness and to practise justice and righteousness.

> "May his [i.e., David's] name endure forever; may it continue as long as the sun. Then all nations will be blessed through him, and they will call him blessed."
> **(Psalm 72:17)**

Notice how this verse refocuses the hopes of the covenant with Abraham (to bless the nations) through the figure of the king. God would bring about His purposes for Israel – and in so doing, the world – through David's royal descendants. In addition, God Himself came to live among His people in the Jerusalem Temple.

> **How would you explain the idea of 'covenant' to someone who asked you? Can you identify one main feature of the Abraham, Sinai, and Davidic covenants?**

NOTES

Episode 5: Exile and the Death of Israel

Though loved and blessed by the One True God, Israel wandered from Him, pursuing other gods and forgetting His ways. God remained patient with His people, despite nearly 500 years of disobedience, but their actions did have consequences. God sent His prophets to warn His people of what their sin would cost. They warned the people that a disaster was coming. According to Israel's prophets, the reasons for that coming disaster boiled down to three main problems: Idolatry (worshipping other gods and powers), immorality, and injustice. For these three things, Israel's Kingdom would face ruin.

And so it did. Tragically, Israel's Kingdom split into a Northern Kingdom (which retained the name 'Israel'), and a Southern Kingdom (Judah). The Northern Kingdom was eventually destroyed by the Assyrians in 722BC, and the South was decimated in 587BC. King Nebuchadnezzar of Babylon destroyed Jerusalem and the Temple, and exiled many Israelites to Babylon.

Everything that made Israel a nation was ruined - its Temple, land, king, and unity. God's presence abandoned the Temple (Ezekiel 8-10) and the people were scattered far and wide throughout the Babylonian Empire. Israel had come full circle. It had returned back to the place from which their ancestor Abraham had been called!

Israel's exile was a kind of national death. The nation became desperately poor, leaderless, and scattered. But the greatest crisis was spiritual. Was God going to remain faithful to His covenants? Had he abandoned His people? The book of Lamentations (after Jeremiah) expresses these painful questions with brutal honesty and grief, and gives voice to the pain and affliction of the now-devastated city of Jerusalem:

> "Her fall was astounding; there was none to comfort her. 'Look, LORD, on my affliction, for the enemy has triumphed.' The enemy laid hands on all her treasures; she saw pagan nations enter her sanctuary – those you had forbidden to enter your assembly. All her people groan as they search for bread; they barter their treasures for food to keep themselves alive. 'Look, LORD, and consider, for I am despised.'" **(Lamentations 1:9-11)**

Feel the weight of that cry for a moment.

The Babylonians had dealt a mortal blow to Israel, and with it, the prospect of any rescue for all humanity. If Israel was God's solution to humanity's crisis, and Israel had effectively died, then all humanity was without hope. The book of Lamentations ends with a desperate plea:

> "Restore us to yourself, LORD, that we may return; renew our days as of old, unless you have utterly rejected us and are angry with us beyond measure."
> **(Lamentations 5:21-22)**

With dashed hopes and only a thread of faith, the story almost came to an abrupt end.

 *Has anything happened to you that has left you feeling hopeless or as if everything is ruined? You might want to bring this to God in 'lament.' Lamenting means bringing your disappointments and grief to God, telling Him honestly what is wrong. Talk with your mentor about how to bring your outcry (or someone else's) to God, and perhaps even write down your own lament.*

NOTES

Speaking in darkness: The hope of the prophets

When all seemed lost, the people were left with two options. Either they could give up and bury all their former hopes, or they could continue to cry out to God. They chose the latter path. And in their crying out, God raised up prophets of hope, prophets like Isaiah, Jeremiah, and Ezekiel (you can read about them in the Old Testament books by those names). These prophets began to paint pictures of hope with their words. They spoke of a coming day, when all things would be restored, when the people would again return to their land, enjoy its fruits, and their children would play unharmed in the streets.

All of these visions of hope raised a fundamental question. If the people returned to the land, what would keep them from reverting back to their old ways? What would keep them from idolatry, immorality, and injustice? One of the answers to these questions is that God would make a **New Covenant** with the people. This covenant would be similar to the Sinai Covenant ... but different. This time God would remake His covenant *partners* so that they would be able to keep God's law. God said, 'I will give you a new heart and put a new spirit in you; I will remove from you your heart of stone and give you a heart of flesh' (Ezekiel 36:26). God said He would then take this new heart and write His law upon it, 'And I will be their God and they will be my people' (Jeremiah 31:33).

Disappointed again

But when would this happen? After about 50 years in exile, some of the people were allowed to return to their homeland Israel. The books of Ezra and Nehemiah talk about this return. The people began rebuilding Jerusalem's walls, its Temple, and their lives. But this did not turn out as hoped. When the people saw the rebuilt Temple, some of the older generation who remembered the old Temple (built by Solomon) wept (Ezra 3:12). Later, we learn that the returnees had to give most of their land's yield to the ruling Persians, and were even forced to sell their children as slaves (Nehemiah 5:5). Again they cried out:

> "But see, we are slaves today, slaves in the land you gave our ancestors so they could eat its fruit and the other good things it produces." **(Nehemiah 9:36)**

The hoped-for restoration looked nothing like it was supposed to. The disappointment was now doubly intense. Not only had the people lost everything; they had also seen their rekindled hopes dashed again on the rocks of slavery. Returning to the land was supposed to be like returning to the Garden of Eden: a place of freedom, bounty, and joy - a place of *shalom*. Instead, it was imprisonment.

So it is with a desperate cry and unfulfilled hopes that the Old Testament ends. How will God intervene to redeem His people?

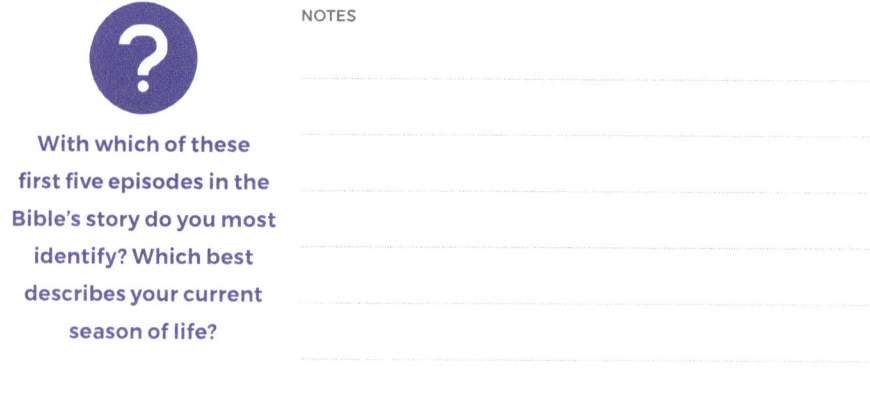

With which of these first five episodes in the Bible's story do you most identify? Which best describes your current season of life?

NOTES

NOTES

The Bible:

Old Testament Books

HISTORICAL BOOKS
THE PAST

- Genesis
- Exodus
- Leviticus
- Numbers
- Deuteronomy
- Joshua
- Judges
- Ruth
- 1 & 2 Samuel
- 1 & 2 Kings
- 1 & 2 Chronicles
- Ezra
- Nehemiah
- Esther

POETIC BOOKS
THE PRESENT

- Job
- Psalms
- Proverbs
- Ecclesiastes
- Songs of Songs
- Lamentations

PROPHETIC BOOKS
THE FUTURE

- Isaiah
- Jeremiah
- Ezekiel
- Daniel
- Hosea
- Joel
- Amos
- Obadiah
- Jonah
- Micah
- Nahum
- Habakkuk
- Zephaniah
- Haggai
- Zechariah
- Malachi

An Overview

New Testament Books

GOSPELS
JESUS
- Matthew
- Mark
- Luke
- John

THE EARLY CHURCH
- Acts

EPISTLES/LETTERS
THE CHURCH

- Romans
- 1 & 2 Corinthians
- Galatians
- Ephesians
- Philippians
- Colossians
- 1 & 2 Thessalonians
- 1 & 2 Timothy
- Titus
- Philemon
- Hebrews
- James
- 1 & 2 Peter
- 1, 2, 3 John
- Jude

THE PERSECUTED CHURCH
- Revelation

SESSION 4
A Surprising Deliverance

The first four books of the New Testament are called 'Gospels.' The word 'Gospel' means **Good News**.

**Mark 1; Luke 2:1-20
Matthew 27-28
Revelation 22**

Setting the stage

The Old Testament ends in disappointment (Episode 5) and leaves an important question hanging: will God really redeem? God's answer would come, but it would be many years. A great deal happened in those years, between the time of the last book of the Old Testament (Malachi) and the first book of the New Testament (Matthew). But for our purposes, the main development was that the people of God grew more numerous and more frustrated in the land to which they had returned. There were around one million Jews living in the regions of Judea, Samaria and Galilee when Jesus was born (around 4BC). They lived under heavy taxes, a corrupt Temple system, and a ruthless local leadership, and all this under Roman occupation.

Yet, there were rumours of change circulating. These rumours were started by Israel's (Old Testament) prophets, and they continued to build and grow: Yes, the people were under the thumb of Rome, the most powerful kingdom on earth, yet a day was coming when one of David's descendants would redeem the people from oppression and return to the throne. The Temple was indeed controlled by a corrupt group of priests, but God's presence would one day return and purify Israel's worship.

The human heart was still rebellious and sinful, but God would give His people a new heart, one that kept true to His ways. The nations were walking in darkness, yet one day, the prophets said, a great light would dawn upon them from Jerusalem. And even though creation was groaning under oppression, the prophets told of a day when God's Spirit-empowered image-bearers would again rule with God. In short, God would one day re-establish His Kingdom on earth.

Read and discover
- God will give a new heart (Jeremiah 31:31-34; Ezekiel 11:19)
- A great light will dawn (Isaiah 9:1-7)
- God's Spirit-empowered image-bearers will rule (Ezekiel 11:17-20; 36:22-30)

Many of us are holding on to hope that our circumstances will change. Is this true for you? Think about sharing your hopes with God in prayer.

NOTES

Episode 6: Jesus and the Church

Israel's hopes were bold; but would God *really* make good on all His promises? The answer was Yes! … but not how they expected. Jesus was God's answer to the hopes of His people and the nations. Let us look at how the story of Jesus unfolded, and what that means for us today.

The Gospel announcement

The first four books of the New Testament are called *Gospels*. The word 'gospel' means **Good News**. Jesus came to announce 'the good news,' but what was this news? One of our first clues comes in the beginning of Luke's Gospel. An angel, accompanied by a whole angelic army, visited a few poor shepherds of Bethlehem to announce the birth of Jesus:

> "I bring you **good** news that will cause great joy for all the people. Today in the **town of David** a Saviour has been born to you; he is the **Messiah, the Lord**." **(Luke 2:10-11)**

This announcement sounds about as many royal notes as possible in two sentences. It concerned a place, the 'town of David' (Bethlehem) which was the birthplace of Israel's beloved king of old. The reference to David must have instantly awakened hopes for a king. This king was 'Saviour,' which to these shepherds probably suggested that this royal baby might deliver Israel from the Roman occupation. He was also 'Messiah' and 'Lord.' Messiah simply means 'anointed one.' It was usually kings who were anointed - or picked by God - in the Old Testament. So by virtue of being the Messiah, he was worthy of being called Lord. In short, *the good news is the announcement that Jesus is king.* This is where the journey began with the shepherds, and where it begins with us as well. We hear the Good News that Jesus is our king, Lord, and Saviour.

Think about what it means to have Jesus as the King, Lord, and Saviour of your life.

NOTES

The shepherds' response

The shepherds' response to this Good News provides us with a good example: 'When they had seen him, they spread the word concerning what had been told them about this child' (Luke 2:17). They could not help but circulate the news when hearing first-hand that Israel's king had been born. Luke tells us that everyone who heard 'wondered at' what they said. Their wonder likely led them back to the promises of the prophets. Could *he* be the one to restore the kingdom to Israel?

Write down the name of someone you know who needs to hear the Good News of Jesus. Pray for them with your mentor and discuss concrete plans for sharing the Good News with them.

Jesus gathers his disciples

When Jesus began his public ministry as an adult, one of the first things he did was gather twelve disciples, or apprentices, to follow him and learn his ways. This was a deeply symbolic act, since the twelve recalled to the Jewish mind the twelve tribes that made up the people of Israel. They would then carry on his mission to heal the sick and crippled, associate with the poor, and preach the Good News of God's Kingdom.

Following Jesus, learning from him, and living life with him is what discipleship is all about.

Jesus had other followers besides the twelve young men. Many women were among those learning to be his disciples. These disciples came from all walks of life. Being a disciple of Jesus meant not only learning from his teachings, but *doing* the things he did. In one remarkable story Jesus miraculously walked on water, but rather than turning the spotlight on himself, he invited his disciple Peter to get out of the boat and try it for himself (Matthew 14:22-33). As you watch Jesus, think about what he might be asking you to try out for yourself! He is a master who shares his power, who gives it freely, and who invites us to 'step out onto the water' with him.

Think of ways that you find Jesus' life attractive or inviting. Are these things you could try imitating? Think of something you would like to try this week.

NOTES

The crucified king

Because Jesus shared access to the Kingdom of God with outcasts, the political and religious leaders grew increasingly upset. They considered themselves the 'gatekeepers' of the Kingdom, and they wanted status and power for themselves. But Jesus taught that those who forsake their status will be given honour in his Kingdom. He had blessed and identified with the poor, children, women, and foreigners—those who were typically seen as unimportant. He taught that they were best prepared to enter his Kingdom.

In the end, Jesus' Kingdom way proved too threatening for those in power. So they resorted to violence. Here is how it happened:

During the Jewish Passover festival, when the Jews celebrated their freedom from the oppressive power of Egypt, Jesus rode into Jerusalem on a humble donkey. For Jews who knew the Old Testament, this was Jesus' way of telling the people that he was Israel's King (see Zechariah 9:9).

The religious leaders feared that an uprising would take place, since the crowds loved Jesus. So they arrested him at night, after a tip-off from one of Jesus' trusted friends, named Judas. They then mocked Jesus by 'crowning' him with thorns, clothed him with a purple robe as they tortured him, and then crucified him. They placed a sign above his head with the words 'King of the Jews.' They meant to mock. But they had killed their true king with the most dishonourable death anyone could endure.

Most onlookers only saw the humiliating execution of a would-be king. But in reality, the crucifixion was the greatest revelation of God's glory (John 13:31-32), because on the cross Jesus defeated all the sin, evil, and death that had afflicted the world since Eden. He put them to death in himself, and in so doing, set us free from all that afflicts us.

At the heart of this victory, shockingly, Jesus forgave his enemies (Luke 23:24), before he breathed his last breath and declared that his work was 'finished' (John 19:30). The Messiah - King Jesus – won his greatest victory by dying! It is not surprising that Paul, a Jewish convert to Christianity who became one the most important leaders of the early church, said, 'The foolishness of God is wiser than human wisdom, and the weakness of God is stronger than human strength' (1 Corinthians 1:25).

As Christians, we see the victory of King Jesus amidst the dishonour of his death. Jesus' death stands at the centre of the Christian faith and life. Paul has spelled out its significance for us:

"When you were dead in your sins ... God made you alive with Christ. He forgave us all our sins, having cancelled the charge of our legal indebtedness, which stood against us and condemned us; he has taken it away, nailing it to the cross." **(Colossians 2:13-14)**

But for Jesus' disciples, his death seemed like a tragedy. From their point of view, it looked like their king had been defeated. But he had not. Three days later, God raised Jesus from the dead! He was resurrected, demonstrating without a doubt *that the victory of the cross had been achieved*. This wonderful news was first announced to women (Matt 28:1-8), who then proclaimed it to the other disciples. The news soon spread like wildfire.

What is the significance of Jesus' crucifixion? Why do you think the resurrection mattered?

NOTES

The Spirit and the Church

After his resurrection and various encounters with his followers, Jesus 'ascended into heaven.' It might sound like he launched into outer space and is now gone, but his *ascension* really means that Jesus ascended to the throne as King over creation. It is precisely the opposite of leaving. The King has *returned* and now rules. Even though he is not visibly present in the world, he is present through his Holy Spirit (sometimes called the Spirit of Jesus) to his followers – the Church. The Spirit of Jesus enables disciples to become changed, gathered, and empowered to carry on his work to 'the ends of the earth' (Acts 1:8).

The giving of his Spirit happened on a day called Pentecost. Pentecost is an ancient Jewish harvest festival, but for Christians, it is remembered as the day when the Holy Spirit came in power upon a group of Jewish believers gathered in Jerusalem (Acts 2). They were filled with the Spirit and all of a sudden began to speak in 'tongues,' which on that occasion meant various languages. Every visitor who was in Jerusalem for the festival understood the Good News of Jesus in their own language. They were then able to share that news in their own culture.

This is how King Jesus rules. He shares his power with *you* so that *you* can be transformed and can tell the story of Jesus through the example of your life. The transformation that the Holy Spirit brings is so powerful that, as one New Testament writer puts it: 'If anyone is in Christ, *there is* New Creation' (2 Corinthians 5:17).

The big idea

You are a New Creation, adopted into the family of God and deeply loved by the Father. In this way, God is at work, creating a people (you and your Christian community) and a place (your neighbourhood) for His presence (in and through you).

One of the most significant ways that you can cooperate with the Spirit's work in your life is by heeding Jesus' call to die to yourself. Jesus called his disciples to leave their old lives to follow him, to 'die' to the old and live in the new. He calls all of his followers to 'take up your cross daily' (Luke 9:23). In part, this means being prepared to let the things that stand in the way of your relationship with him die. It can be painful to let some things go, but what we gain in return is *always* worth it. With Jesus, the promise of new life and resurrection is always ahead.

Pray and ask God to help you yield to His Spirit.

An unfinished story

The final episode (New Creation) has only just begun. New Creation is breaking into this hurting world but has not yet arrived in all its glory. Before we talk about this final episode, however, let us reflect more closely on what it means to be a disciple of Jesus. The next two sessions will explore this new life you now have, before turning our attention to the end of the story.

SESSION 4

What does life between Episode 6 (Jesus) and Episode 7 (New Creation) look like? Are there any ways that you feel new *and* like an unfinished work?

NOTES

Notes

SESSION 5

Following The Master

Some people think that becoming a Christian is about following a set of rules, but there are only two rules: Love God and love your neighbour.

SESSION 5

Matthew 5-7

Perfect freedom

"Everyone who hears these words of mine and puts them into practice is like a wise man who built his house on the rock. The rain came down, the streams rose, and the winds blew and beat against that house; yet it did not fall, because it had its foundation on the rock." **(Matthew 7:24-25)**

These words of Jesus, spoken at the end of his most famous teaching, the Sermon on the Mount, show us the practice and the value of discipleship. When we put his teaching into practice, we feel like we are standing on solid ground, even when storms rage. This is what it looks like to follow him.

Jesus also teaches his disciples that following his teachings sets people free. He brings freedom and deliverance (Luke 4:16-19). So while Jesus taught a great deal about how we should live, living by those teachings set us free. They break the chains of sin and evil that hold us captive. This is why Jesus spent far more time emphasising what is *permitted* than what is *prohibited*.

Yet many people think that becoming a Christian is about following a set of rules. Really, there are only two rules: Love God with everything you are, and love your neighbour as you love yourself (Matthew 22:37-40). Working that out well in our lives will keep most of us busy forever! Doing God's will sets us free. That is the power of following His teachings.

"If the Son sets you free, you will be free indeed." **(John 8:36)**

When Jesus says that he sets us free, what is he setting us free from?

NOTES

Following rules can become burdensome and exhausting. Jesus promises the opposite. He says, 'Come to me, all you who are weary and burdened, and I will give you rest' (Matthew 11:28). He is the opposite of a taskmaster. He is gentle and humble in heart, and he promises that following him will be like the lifting of a heavy burden.

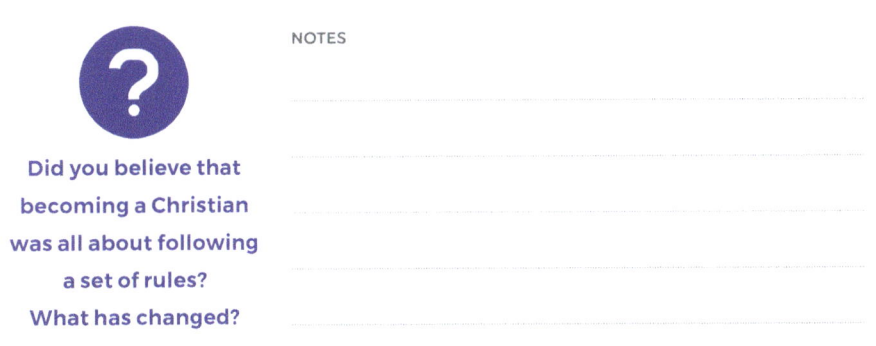

Did you believe that becoming a Christian was all about following a set of rules? What has changed?

NOTES

Loving communities

God's vision is for us to become communities of people who love God with our whole hearts and love each other like He loves us. As we do, His church will become an amazingly attractive place, full of healing, reconciliation, and peace. We know the church is not always like this, but it is possible for people to love one another in this way when our hearts are touched by God. And when we love each other as Jesus loves us, people on the outside will look in and want to experience that love for themselves. This is the best way to be an ambassador for Jesus.

Think of someone you can share God's love with by doing something kind for them.

NOTES

Desiring the best

Jesus told his disciples that if they really loved him, they would obey his teaching (John 14:23), but Christians do not always obey Jesus and we do not always put his words into practice. Nevertheless, when we tell him we *want* to do this, he always helps us to follow him and to be able to do what he asks us to do. What counts is our obedience to our relationship with Jesus, not an abstract list of rules.

Faith begins by deciding that we want to follow Jesus and to put his words into practice, even if we are not always able to follow that through. To help us, God has given us His words, His Holy Spirit, and friends who will support us. It is important that we make sure to use them all!

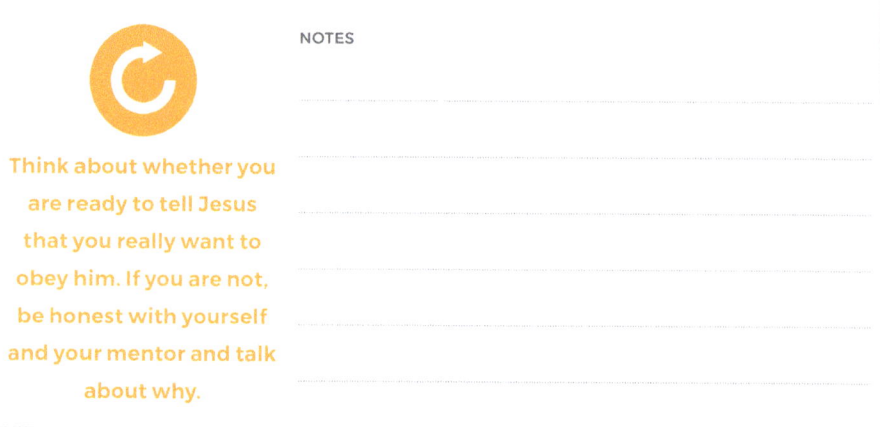

Think about whether you are ready to tell Jesus that you really want to obey him. If you are not, be honest with yourself and your mentor and talk about why.

NOTES

A good deal

We are not on our own in the Christian life, and even more importantly, God is now living in us by His Spirit. He helps us and changes us from the inside. God makes an exchange: We give our lives to Him, and He gives Himself to us, to make us like Him. We give Him the good and the bad, the beautiful and the ugly, the joys and the sadnesses, the successes and the failures, and He gives us His own goodness, His own love, His own holiness, and more besides. He gives us His Spirit and through the gift of His Spirit,

He begins to make us like His Son, Jesus. This is the journey that you have begun. This is all part of becoming a disciple, a Christian.

What does that exchange mean to you?

NOTES

Being filled with the Spirit

The best way that God helps us is by filling us with His Holy Spirit. All we have to do is ask. Everyone who knows that Jesus is Lord has the gift of the Holy Spirit. We know that no-one can claim and believe that Jesus is Lord unless the Holy Spirit is working in them, but the Bible tells us to 'keep on being filled with the Spirit' (Ephesians 5:18).

In the same way that we maintain a constant intake of food and water to keep us alive and healthy, we need to keep feeding from God's Word by reading the Bible and drinking in His living water, which is the Spirit. This is how we keep re-fuelling.

Because the Holy Spirit is the power and presence of God with us, people sometimes have a dramatic experience when they pray to be filled with the Spirit. They might laugh or cry or feel a warmth or tingling like electricity in their bodies. Sometimes people just feel a sense of peace and rest. Sometimes people feel very little. It does not matter what 'happens'. We know that when we ask to be filled with the Spirit, that God always answers our prayer, and He always gives us good things. He is a loving heavenly Father who only gives His children good gifts (See Luke 11:9-13).

"Every good and perfect gift is from above, coming down from the Father of the heavenly lights, who does not change like shifting shadows." **(James 1:17)**

 **Pray and ask God to fill you with His Spirit.**

Forgiving others

In the Lord's Prayer (p. 9) we say, "Forgive us our sins as we forgive those who sin against us." You might have been brought up saying, "Forgive us our trespasses ..." or "Forgive us our debts ..."

In Matthew 6:14-15 Jesus goes so far as to say that if we do not forgive our enemies, then God will not forgive us. This is not a threat, but to show us how seriously God takes the issue of forgiveness. Refusing to forgive other people is like a sign to Him that we have not really understood yet how much we have been forgiven.

Once we know how merciful God has been to us, we cannot withhold that mercy from other people. If we do, we will also harden our hearts to God.

Making peace with your enemies

There are many people in the world who hurt us and damage us and many people who we hurt and damage. Some may have deliberately hurt us, and we may have deliberately hurt others. Whereas other relationships may simply have gone wrong.

Whatever has happened to us, and whatever we have done, we all come to Jesus with a mixture of emotions. We may feel deeply grateful that he has forgiven us; we may feel great relief that our burdens have been lifted off us - the burdens of guilt and shame. This is what Jesus promises to do. We all need forgiveness and mercy from others, and we all need to forgive those who have hurt us. Sometimes all we can do is to seek and offer forgiveness. This can lead to reconciliation, where we find peace in our relationships.

But we may also feel anger at some people for what they have done to us, or regret for the things we have done, or sadness over the past, and a desire to make some things right. We cannot always make everything right in all our past or current relationships, and healing can take a very long time in some cases, but we can begin a process of forgiveness and reconciliation.

If you find it hard to forgive, confess that to God and to someone else. Ask for God's help. Do not be discouraged if it takes a long time and the pain and anger keeps coming back. Jesus said we might need to forgive the same person up to seventy times seven. At least he was realistic!

Think about who you still need to forgive and talk this through with your mentor.

If you need forgiveness from others, and it is possible to approach them about it, talk to your mentor about the best way to do this. Speaking face-to-face or writing a letter to say sorry and to ask for their forgiveness is best, but however you are able to do this will be a good start.

Sorting out relationships

The Bible gives us two pictures of intimate relationships for Christians: *marriages* between men and women, and *family* (brothers and sisters, parents and children). If we are married, then we make a covenant or promise to be with that person our whole lives until death parts us. Anyone we are not married to is supposed to be like a brother or sister or parent or child. But not all our relationships fall into either one of these categories, especially if we have only recently become a Christian. The model of relationships in the Bible sets the bar high and this can feel intimidating (even for people who have been Christians for a long time!), but remember that most of all, God wants to *be* with you, whatever your situation.

People come to know God from all kinds of different backgrounds. A lot of people who join the church are living with or sleeping with people they are not married to, or have already been married and divorced. Some people are in very loving relationships, but probably most people come with regrets and sadness about what they have done before they knew God. In addition to this, a lot of people have been involved with porn, and when they start to realise the effect this has had on them, this causes shame and guilt. It often takes a long time to work through past and present relationships with God. The most important thing is that everyone knows they are always welcome in God's house, so the first thing to do is to find a church that makes you welcome for who you are.

After that, find someone you can trust to talk through how you are feeling and where you are in your relationships. Is there anything you would like to be different? If so, remember that change can be disorientating for those who love us and who might feel that they have lost us to Jesus. Take time to explain to your loved ones what is going on and why.

In the Sermon on the Mount, we have read about how Jesus wants us to treat others - lovingly and without anger, lust, or manipulation. If there are things that you would like to change in any of your relationships or habits, remember that it can take time and help from others to break habits and dependencies that have formed, but that Jesus is always with you and in you, and he is your greatest supporter.

Talk to your mentor or group about how to go about bringing your relationships in line with God's patterns for us, and remember that Jesus is in you by the Holy Spirit to help you.

NOTES

Telling others

Whatever happens, do not wait until you think you are perfect to start telling others about Jesus because a) you will never be perfect, and b) sharing the good news with other people is all part of how we *start* to change. Remember, we are living *between* the time of Jesus' victory and the fullness of New Creation. We are a work in progress. God has given us *His* holiness, so that when He looks at us He sees us as perfect, even though, as the writer of Hebrews tells us, we are still 'being made holy' (2:11). We have not yet fully arrived.

In the next session, we will look at good habits to form, the gifts that God gives us, and how we can use them to bless others, before looking at the final episode of the biblical story.

Another word for 'disciple' is 'apprentice.' Believers are apprentices of Jesus in the family business of the Kingdom of Heaven. As an apprentice, what is the one area of the business of the Kingdom of Heaven that you most want to grow in?

The big idea
Following the master
- *Perfect freedom*
- *Loving communities*
- *Desiring the best*
- *A good deal*
- *Being filled with the Spirit*
- *Forgiving others*
- *Making peace with your enemies*
- *Sorting out relationships*
- *Telling others*

SESSION 6

New Habits, New Gifts, and a New Me

Learning to live like a Christian is how we respond to God's gift to us, and this takes effort.

1 Peter 1:3-2:3
2 Peter 1:3-11
Ephesians 1-2

Making an effort

Becoming a Christian can happen in a moment, but it also takes a lifetime. You have become a new creation; God has filled you with His Spirit; and Jesus has made his home in you so that you might become like him. You have been forgiven of *all* that you have done wrong and a new life lies ahead of you. You are holy already because God has given you His holiness, and you are being made holy by God's Spirit. It is as if we are all learning to become what we have been given.

In 2 Peter 1:3, Peter says that God has given us everything we need for life and godliness – everything! But he also says:

"For this very reason, you must make every effort to support your faith with goodness, and goodness with knowledge, and knowledge with self-control, and self-control with endurance, and endurance with godliness, and godliness with mutual affection, and mutual affection with love." **(2 Peter 1:5-7, NRSV)**

The faith that you have is a gift from God. Learning to live like a Christian is how we respond to God's gift to us, and it takes effort. This means exerting our energy to keep moving along the path He has laid out for us, and it means being active in making good and wise decisions, so that we do not get derailed by life.

Listening to His voice

You will be praying already. Prayer is telling God everything that is on your mind and listening to Him. Sometimes we come to God with lists of things we are worried about. That is okay, but let Him speak too, and let the Holy Spirit give you prayers to pray. Sometimes these prayers come from our Bible reading and sometimes they come as ideas into our heads: "I should pray for her, or this, or that." Sometimes God speaks very specifically to us through the Bible or in pictures, dreams, or phrases. The Bible calls this the gift of prophecy. This gift is wonderful when praying for others, and sometimes we can share with them what we think God is saying.

Start keeping a prayer journal so that you can record all of your answers to prayer. This can be a great encouragement to keep praying and not give up!

[Jesus said] "My sheep listen to my voice; I know them, and they follow me." **(John 10:27)**

Resisting the enemy of our faith

Jesus and all the writers of the New Testament knew that our faith would come under attack. Whatever other people do to us, Christians should never see other people as enemies. Paul writes that we do not have enemies of flesh and blood, but that there are forces that come against us, seeking to destroy our faith, our peace, and our joy. We can easily become convinced that God will not keep His promises, and if we lose sight of Him, we can fall away.

The Bible names these forces that come against our faith as: Satan, the devil, the prince of this world, principalities and powers, our sinful natures, our worldly desires, and our own flesh.

In other words, these influences are in the world around us, in our cultures and values, and in ourselves and our own selfish desires. God gives us weapons to fight the battle: the Word of God in the Bible, so that we know His promises; the Holy Spirit's power in us, so that we know who we are in God; the peace of God; confession; and praise and worship. All of these will help us when we feel that our faith is under attack.

Remember Jesus Christ has defeated all the powers of darkness and lives in you, and that "He who is in you is greater than he who is in the world." (1 John 4:4)

Repent of any times you have agreed with anything that you can now see was actively evil. Receive God's forgiveness for that and know that you are protected from it from now on.

Keep moving on

Growing and maturing as a Christian means that we have to keep moving forward. Some Christians stop moving and growing, but if you do then life becomes dull and becoming a Christian gets hard. God will always be in us, moving us towards Him, but if we do not respond then it can be like standing still on a mile-long travelator (a moving walkway). You may get to the end eventually, but it will take ages, your legs will get tired, and the journey will be boring. But as soon as you start to walk, with the help of the travelator, you will cover ground quickly and easily. When we move, God's Spirit helps us to do more than we can do on our own. Partnering with Him in the Kingdom is exciting, dynamic, and full of surprises. With God, the journey is never dull!

Here are some ways of engaging with God's plans in the Kingdom:

Share your faith

Telling people about your faith changes you and them at the same time. You do not need to wait to be perfect or to try and tell your story exactly the way you want to! Just tell people what has happened and why you decided to give your life to Jesus. Tell them about the difference he has made to you and let them know that a relationship with him is for everyone who turns to him.

If you have not been baptised yet, start to plan your baptism, invite all of your friends, and ask your minister or pastor if you can tell your story as a part of that.

Serve in the Church and in the world

Christians have a mandate from God to look after the vulnerable in society. Maybe you and your family are the vulnerable ones and it was Christians who helped you. Or maybe you have everything you could ever need. Whether we are privileged or under-privileged, rich or poor, God wants us to give to others in any way that we can. It helps us to become more loving and thoughtful of others, and it demonstrates God's love in concrete ways. Churches are meant to be places where no-one is in need. So if you can use your time, money, or resources to help others, then do.

If you work, ask God how He wants you to be an ambassador for Him at work. Christians in the workplace can be effective agents for change. Prayer for your company and colleagues, and behaving with integrity, can have a powerful effect.

Talk to your mentor or group about plans for financial giving and helping others.

Get some good habits

All of us need to learn how to change our ways when we become Christians, and this is what takes a lifetime! But God helps us to do this in lots of ways. These are called 'spiritual disciplines' or 'holy habits'. We recommend trying to make time to read/listen to the Bible and to pray every day. It is probably best in the morning. If you leave it until last thing at night, you might fall asleep! But any time is better than no time. Maybe you work best reading with a friend or partner. Consider also undertaking some study in the form of a course in theology and the Bible.

Talk with your mentor about Bible study and reading/listening plans to help you know where to start.

Boosting your prayer life!

Ask God to give you the gift of tongues. This is a special prayer language to help us pray when we do not always have our own words. Paul calls it the language of angels. It sounds strange to start with, but when you get used to it, it seems normal.

Think about learning how to fast every now and then. Fasting can be a powerful way of drawing close to God and focusing on specific prayer needs at different times. Our rule is "Fast as you can, not as you can't." There is no need to be heroic. It might mean simply skipping lunch to spend an extra half an hour in prayer that day. If you feel God leading you to do longer fasts, then do.

There are lots of other holy habits you can learn. You can withdraw to spend time with God in times of silence, taking time out from the busy pace of life, and turning off your phone for a bit. But being spiritual is not all serious and introverted. Enjoy spending time with others: eat together (feasting), worship together, and make time for laughter and joy.

Why did God create a world where He needed us to partner with Him to get things done?

NOTES

New Habits, New Gifts, and a New Me

Character

God gives us His Son and His Spirit to make us more like Him. There are lots of gifts of the Spirit and you will already have some. Paul told the Corinthian church to make sure that they did not use their spiritual gifts until they knew how to use them in a wholly loving way. Spiritual gifts are given to us so that we can bless other people, not so that we can feel more holy! If we speak in tongues, it is to help us to pray. If we prophesy, it is to give words of encouragement to others that comfort and build them up. If we teach and preach, we have to learn to behave well so that we practice what we preach. If God uses us to bring healing to others, it is not so that we feel powerful but so we can serve in praying for the sick.

> **?**
>
> **What spiritual gifts would you like to grow in? Ask God for those gifts. He loves it when we ask!**
>
> NOTES

A life-long apprenticeship in a team

God loves to involve us as His partners and co-workers in His Kingdom. Imagine being Jesus' close colleague in a project! He tells you what to do and how to do it, and you learn from him. Remember, we are not supposed to be lone rangers, so working as a team is important. Doing things with other Christians is wonderful and testing at the same time. Churches are not perfect places, because they are made up of people who are not yet perfect. Be patient and kind to others and try not to expect too much of them. Resolve conflict quickly, be honest, and don't hold grudges.

This will mean you are an asset to your church! Learn about all the spiritual gifts and think about your own gifting and how God wants to use you. He loves giving us His gifts to help us to live and work in His Kingdom.

Episode 7: New Creation

We return now to the seventh and final episode in the biblical story: when Jesus returns to vanquish all evil and God renews all of creation. We have already described discipleship as becoming an apprentice to Jesus between the time he came to earth and when he returns to make everything new. As you walk with Jesus you will begin to see signs of that coming seventh episode. In fact, *you* are a sign of God's new creation because He has made you new.

Each sign points the way towards the fullness of new creation - of God's Kingdom extended over all the earth. That fuller reality will exceed everything we can imagine. The New Testament uses many images to try and capture that coming reality. Here is one, drawn from a vision seen by the disciple John:

> "*I [John] saw the Holy City, the new Jerusalem, coming down out of heaven from God, prepared as a bride beautifully dressed for her husband ... He [God] will wipe every tear from their eyes. There will be no more death or mourning or crying or pain, for the old order of things has passed away.*" **(Revelation 21:2, 4)**

But until that becomes a reality, we live between the times. On the one hand, Jesus has dealt the death blow against the powers. Yet on the other hand, those powers have not yet fully exhausted themselves. They are crumbling, but have not yet collapsed. The call of discipleship is to leave the crumbling building (generally good advice) and seek the Kingdom.

Life between the times can be difficult and exciting precisely because it involves us in the pain of a failing world and the joyful in-breaking of another. Yet we can have confidence that God *will* make good on His promise to restore creation because of Jesus' resurrection. Paul speaks of Jesus as the 'firstfruits' (or first harvest) of the New Creation (1 Corinthians 15:20), and also says that Jesus has given us the 'firstfruits' of the Spirit (Romans 8:23). In this way, *God will re-create a people and a place for his presence so that all creation can share in His abundant life.*

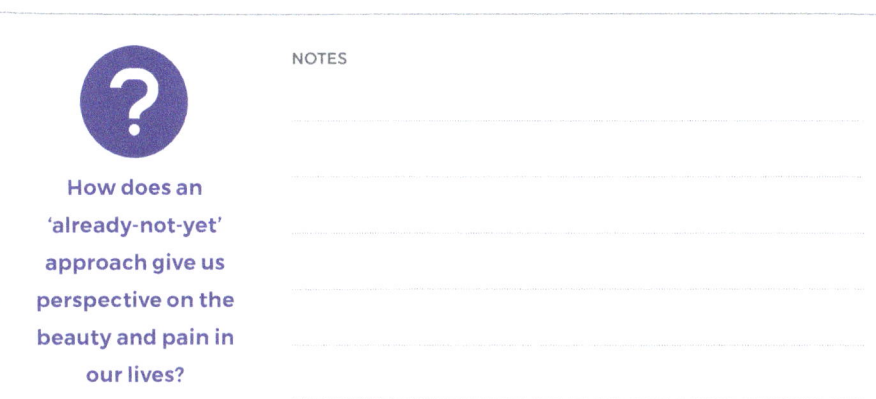

How does an 'already-not-yet' approach give us perspective on the beauty and pain in our lives?

NOTES

Go and make more disciples ...

Until the time of his full return, Jesus calls us to make disciples. In Matthew 28:18-20 we read:

> "Then Jesus came to them and said, 'All authority in heaven and earth has been given to me. Therefore go and make disciples of all nations, baptising them in the name of the Father and of the Son and of the Holy Spirit, and teaching them to obey everything I have commanded you. And surely I am with you always, to the very end of the age.'"

Walking with Jesus and living life with him is the best decision you will ever make. Take a step out of the boat ...

NOTES

www.ingramcontent.com/pod-product-compliance
Lightning Source LLC
Chambersburg PA
CBHW041929040426
42444CB00019B/3475